Introduction

"Little Cooks" shows how to make the favourite dishes of children from all over the world.

The recipes have step by step instructions showing you exactly what to do. Each tasty dish will be enough for four or six people.

Children in their national costumes introduce each recipe, and you can find out where their countries are. Each recipe has a number. The number of the recipe is also the number of the country. Can you find it? For example the Belgian recipe is number one. Just look at the map and find number one and you have found Belgium.

If you turn to the middle of the book, you can find out all about the foods that will help you to grow up strong and healthy.

You can also read about the United Nations Children's Fund which is helping children all over the world.

We hope that you enjoy trying some of the food loved by children the world over.

Acknowledgements

UNICEF wishes to thank everyone who contributed to this book.

15 Practical Pieces of Advice

1 Before you start to cook, wash your hands and put on an apron.

2 Next read the recipe through before you begin.

3 Arrange in front of you all the ingredients and utensils you will need.

4 Make sure you have a damp cloth handy in case you spill something.

5 If you use a knife, always cut downwards onto a board.

6 Remember sharp knives can be dangerous — take care.

7 If you use a pan, do not leave the handle sticking out over the side of the cooker, this will prevent your knocking it over by accident.

8 Use a large bowl resting on the table or bench to mix your ingredients.

9 When using the oven, ask an adult to help you to turn it on.

10 Hold hot dishes or pans with an oven glove or thick cloth — remember to put a mat on the table to rest a hot dish on.

11 Turn off the oven or cooker as soon as your dish is cooked.

12 Arrange your dish to make it look attractive and tempting.

13 Remember to wash up all the pots, pans and utensils you have used when you have finished cooking.

14 Put any rubbish into a bin.

15 If you have a problem, ask an adult for help.

Be careful and have lots of fun!

Cooking Hints

To separate egg whites from yolks:
Put 2 bowls in front of you, one for the whites, the other for the yolks. Tap the egg shell against the side of the bowl for the whites — open the egg with both thumbs and drop the white into one bowl, passing the yolk from one half of the shell into the other.

To stiffen the egg whites:
Put the whites in a bowl and place in refrigerator for 5 minutes; add a pinch of salt before whisking them by hand or with an electric mixer.

To make a cake mixture:
Take the butter out of the refrigerator at least 1 hour ahead so that it is soft and easy to use.

To grease a cake tin:
Put some butter on a piece of greaseproof paper and rub it on the bottom and sides of your tin.

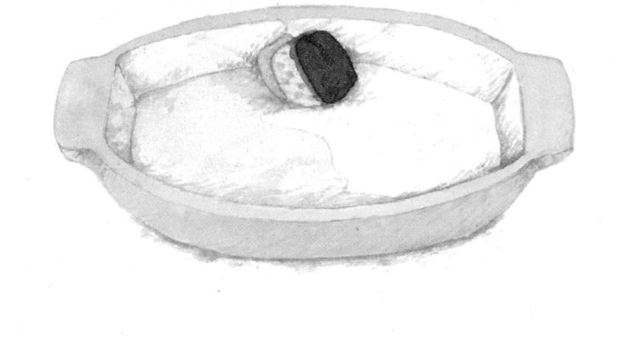

To sift flour:
Pass the flour through a large, fine sieve to get rid of the lumps.

To grate lemon rind:
Wash and wipe the lemon and rub its skin against a fine grater.

To peel an onion:
Peel it under running water and cut it on a damp board, this will stop your eyes watering.

To peel tomatoes:
Scald (boil) them for one minute, put them under the cold tap and the skin will peel off easily.

To chop herbs and parsley:
Cut off the stalks, put the leaves in a narrow glass. Chop them in the glass with some scissors.

To cook rice:
Wash the rice in a colander and then put it into a large pan of boiling salted water, stir until it comes to the boil, then simmer for 15 minutes. Strain through a sieve and then pour hot water over to separate the grains.

Raw Vegetable Fondue

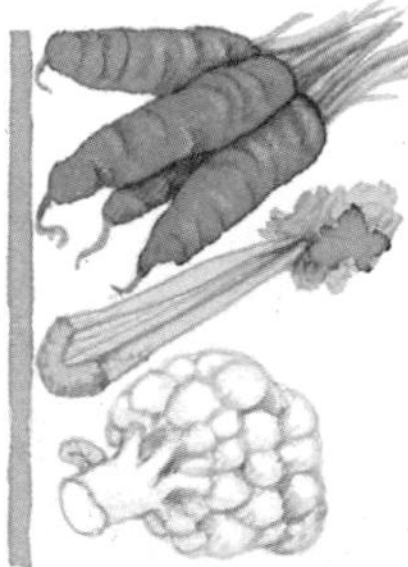

4 carrots

1 stick of celery

1 small cauli-flower

1 medium fennel

1 kale (green curly cabbage)

1 shallot

500 g sieved cottage cheese

3 slices cooked ham

salt, pepper, spices

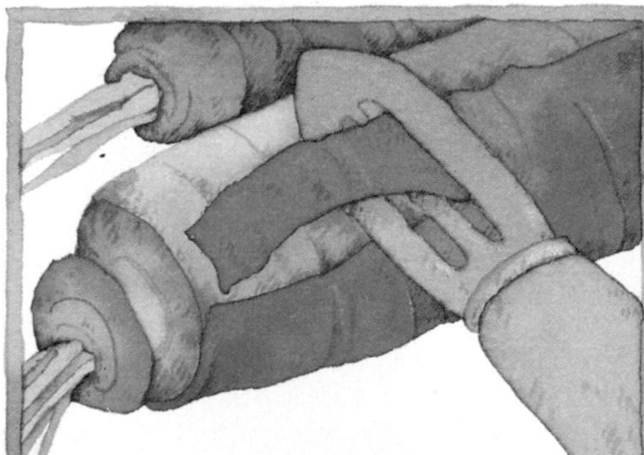

Peel the carrots.

Cut the carrots, celery and fennel into small fingers.

Separate the cauliflower into little florets.

Wash the vegetables in cold water…

…and drain them well.

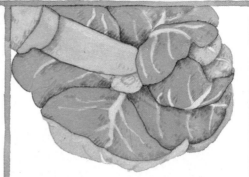

Wash the kale and remove its heart.

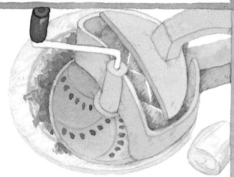

Mince the ham and the shallot…

…and add to the cottage cheese in a small bowl.

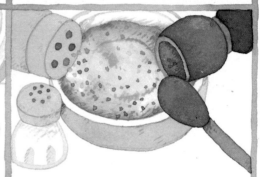

Season with salt, pepper and add the spices.

Put the small bowl in the place of the kale's heart.

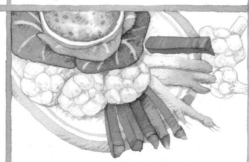

Place the kale on a dish and surround it with the rest of the vegetables.

Your fondue is ready to be served.

Taboulé

250 g crushed wheat

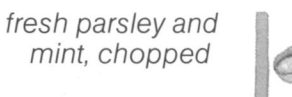 fresh parsley and mint, chopped

8 tablespoons olive oil

500 g washed tomatoes

juice of 3 lemons

150 g stoned black olives

 250 g onions

salt and pepper

 1 tomato, quartered to garnish

Put the wheat into a salad bowl.

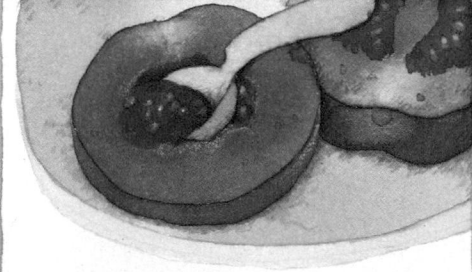

Cut the tomatoes in half and remove the seeds.

Then chop them into small cubes.

Peel the onions under running water…

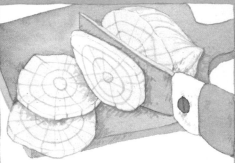

…and cut them into thin slices.

Put the tomatoes, onions, parsley and mint into the salad bowl.

Season with salt and pepper before mixing.

Beat the oil with the lemon juice in a bowl…

…and add to the wheat.

Add the olives.

Chill in the refrigerator for 3 hours.

Serve the taboulé garnished with the tomato quarters.

Vietnamese Salad

300 g cooked shrimps, peeled

200 g cooked chicken breasts

200 g bean sprouts

30 g carrots

½ cucumber

a few coriander leaves

50 g crushed peanuts

2 tablespoons lemon juice

a sprinkle of sugar

2 tablespoons fish sauce ('Nuoc Mam' available from Chinese food shops)

salt and pepper

Boil the water.

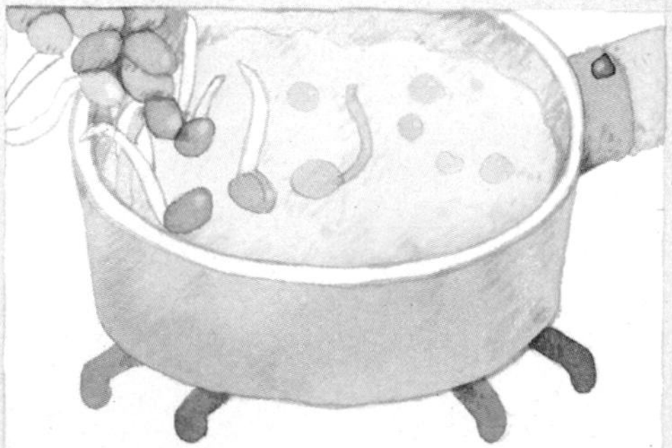

Throw in the bean sprouts for a few seconds only.

Drain and let cool.

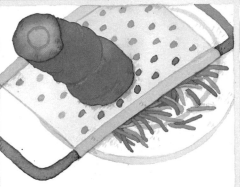

Peel the carrot and the cucumber.

Grate the carrot.

Cut the cucumber into thin slices.

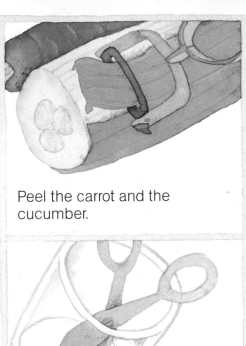

Chop the coriander leaves in a glass with scissors.

Mix the lemon, sugar, fish sauce and pepper in a bowl.

Arrange the vegetables and coriander on a dish and cover with your dressing.

Dice the chicken.

Arrange it with the shrimps on the dish.

Garnish with coriander leaves and crushed peanuts.

Potato Salad

2 medium sized potatoes, boiled

4 hard-boiled eggs

1 cucumber

1 cooking apple

2 medium onions

1 thick slice ham

4 gherkins

4 tablespoons oil

2 tablespoons wine vinegar

salt and pepper

Peel the apple, cucumber and potatoes.

Peel the onions.

Peel the eggs, two of which you will use to garnish your dish.

Cut the remaining eggs in half and remove the yolks.

Mash the yolks separately. Do not mix them together.

Prepare the dressing with one of the yolks, oil, vinegar, salt and pepper.

Dice the apple, potatoes, gherkins, onions, ham and half the cucumber and two cooked egg whites.

Mix all these ingredients with the dressing in a salad bowl.

Chill for 3 hours…

…then garnish it with the remaining cucumber, eggs, and mashed egg-yolk.

Polar Fish

800 g sliced fish fillets (plaice or sole)

1 sprig of parsley

375 ml milk

2½ tablespoons flour

200 g grated cheese

salt and pepper

8 small potatoes

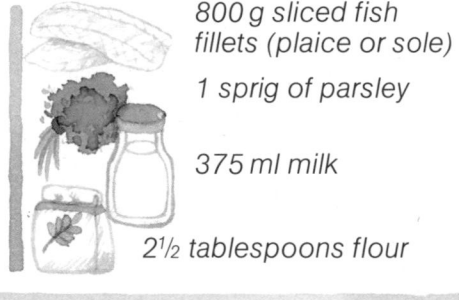

Grease an ovenproof dish.

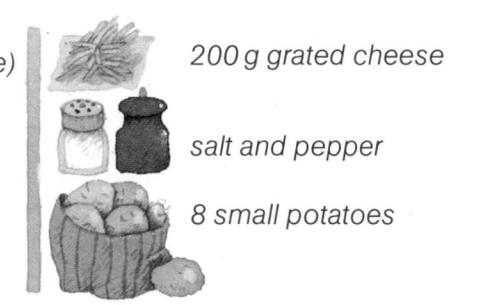

Arrange the fish fillets in the dish.

Chop the parsley in a glass with scissors.

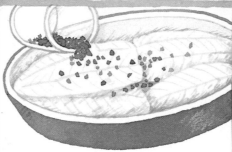

Sprinkle the fillets with the parsley.

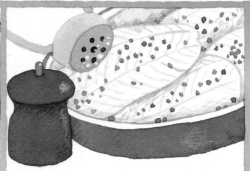

Season with salt and pepper.

Put the flour in a bowl and stir in the milk gradually.

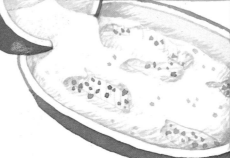

Pour the mixture over the fish.

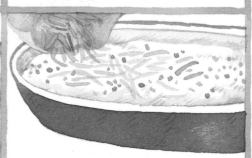

Sprinkle your dish with grated cheese.

Cook in the oven at 220°C for 30 minutes.

In the meantime, boil the potatoes...

...and serve them with your cooked fish.

CYPRUS

Village Salad

 a few washed
lettuce leaves

1 medium onion,
peeled and
chopped

1 big cucumber

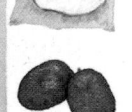 3 medium
tomatoes

50g feta cheese

8 stoned black
olives

 4 tablespoons olive oil

1 tablespoon lemon juice

dried mint

salt

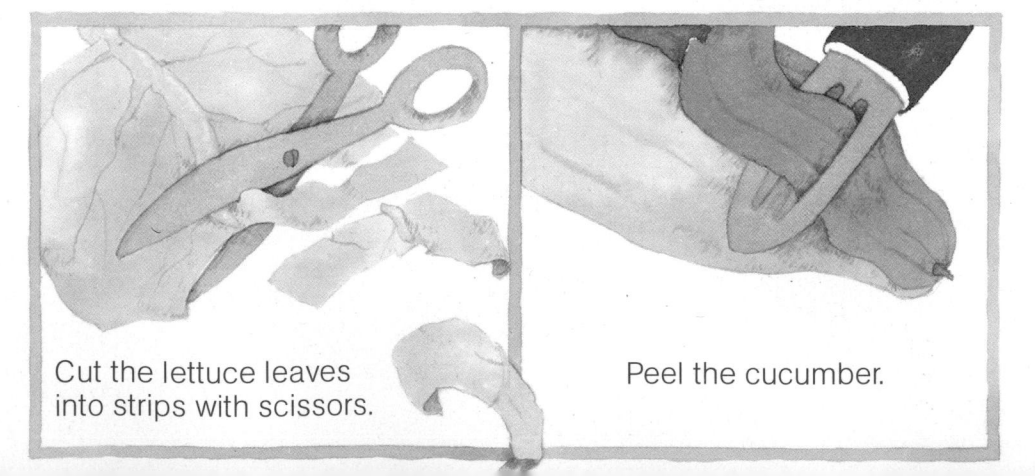

Cut the lettuce leaves
into strips with scissors.

Peel the cucumber.

Chop the cucumber and tomatoes into cubes.

Place the lettuce in a salad bowl…

Add the chopped vegetables and the onion.

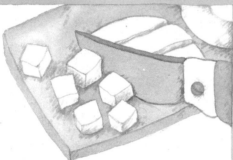

Cut the cheese into small cubes.

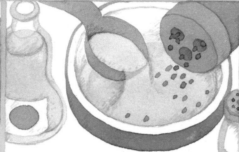

Prepare the dressing with: lemon, oil, mint and salt.

Mix thoroughly.

Pour the dressing into the salad bowl.

Arrange the olives around the side…

…and the cheese in the centre.

Stuffed Tomatoes

For 6 people:

150g crushed wheat

6 big tomatoes

4 small tomatoes

6 small white onions, chopped

Chives

parsley

fresh mint

3 tablespoons olive oil

1 tablespoon lemon juice

salt and pepper

a few washed lettuce leaves

Soak the crushed wheat for 1 hour in cold water until the wheat swells.

Wash the big tomatoes and dry them.

Cut off the top and take out the pulp.

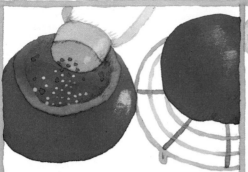

Sprinkle with salt and turn upside down to drain.

Chop the herbs in a glass with scissors.

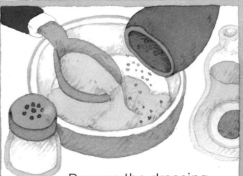

Prepare the dressing with oil, lemon, salt and pepper.

Scald the small tomatoes for 1 minute and then peel.

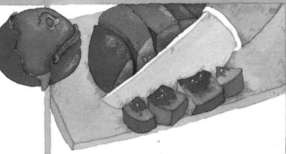

Cut them into cubes.

Strain the wheat.

Mix the tomatoes, wheat, chopped herbs and onions in the dressing.

Fill the large tomatoes with the stuffing…

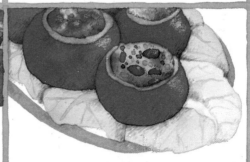

… and arrange them on a bed of lettuce.

Cucumber Salad

1 cucumber

2 small cartons
natural yoghurt

fresh mint

1 clove garlic, chopped

juice of ½ lemon

2 tablespoons olive oil

salt and pepper

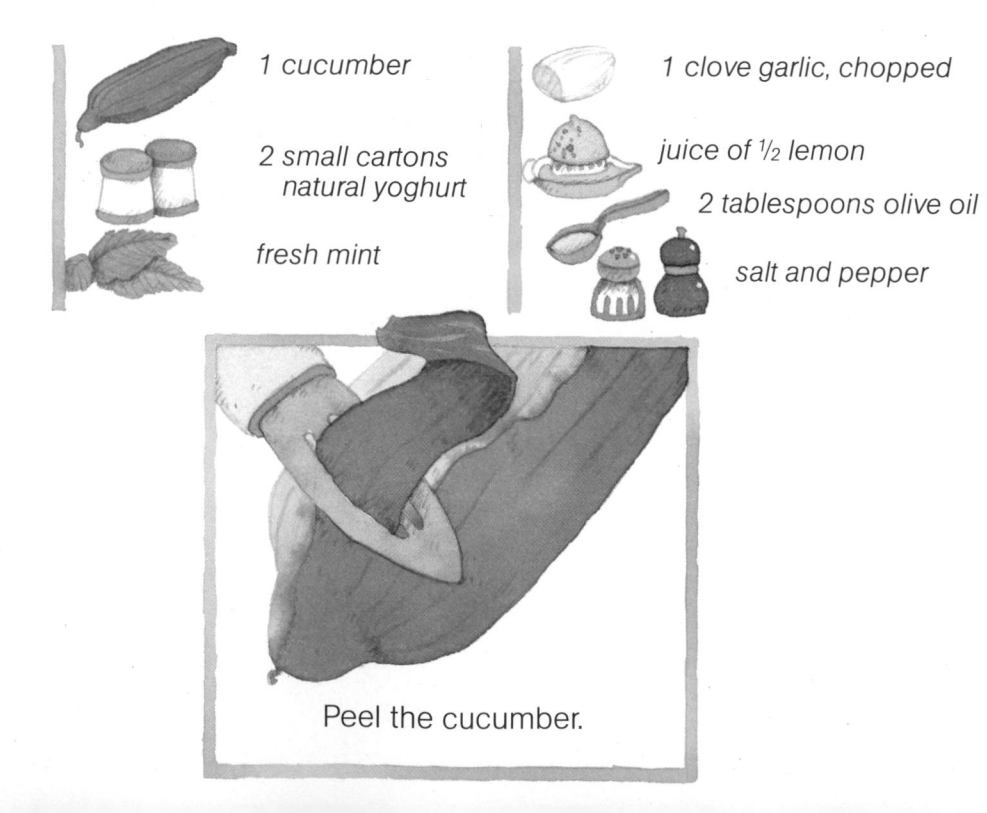

Peel the cucumber.

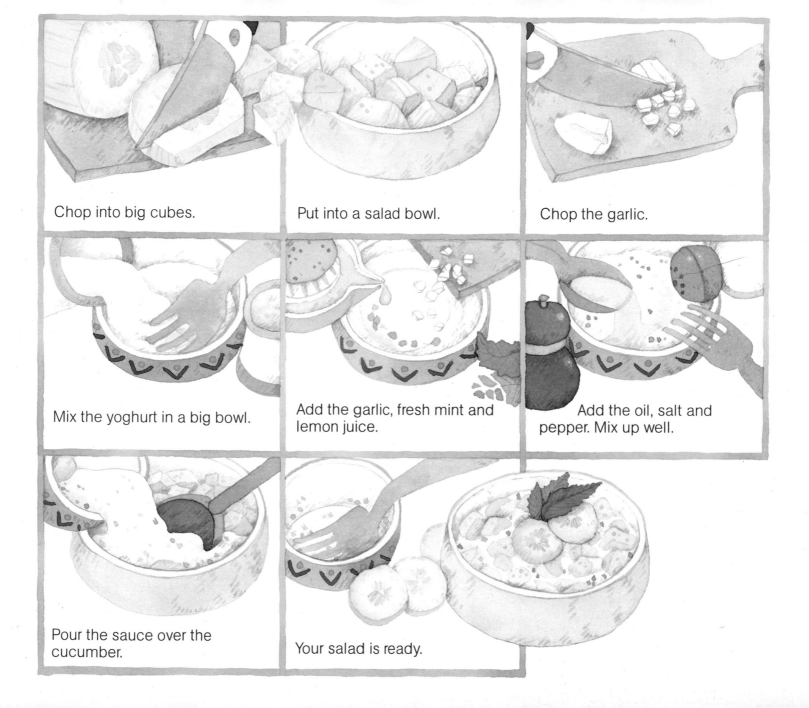

Chop into big cubes.

Put into a salad bowl.

Chop the garlic.

Mix the yoghurt in a big bowl.

Add the garlic, fresh mint and lemon juice.

Add the oil, salt and pepper. Mix up well.

Pour the sauce over the cucumber.

Your salad is ready.

Shrimp with Rice

300 g cooked long grain white rice

180 g shelled shrimps

4 tablespoons sunflower oil

60 g frozen peas

1 beaten egg

2 pinches salt

120 g chopped onion

Heat 2 tablespoons of oil in a pan.

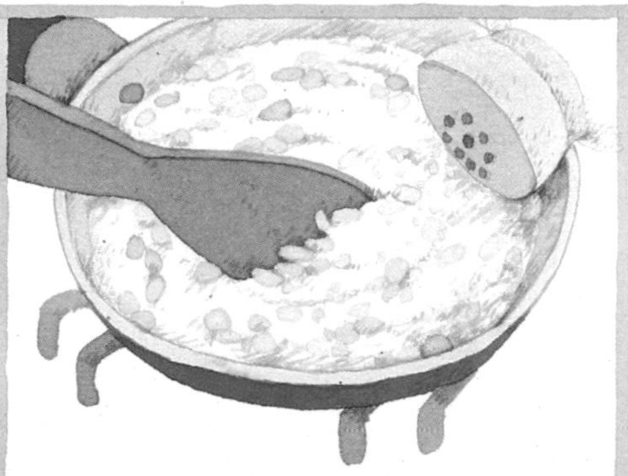

Add the rice and stir with a pinch of salt for 2 minutes.

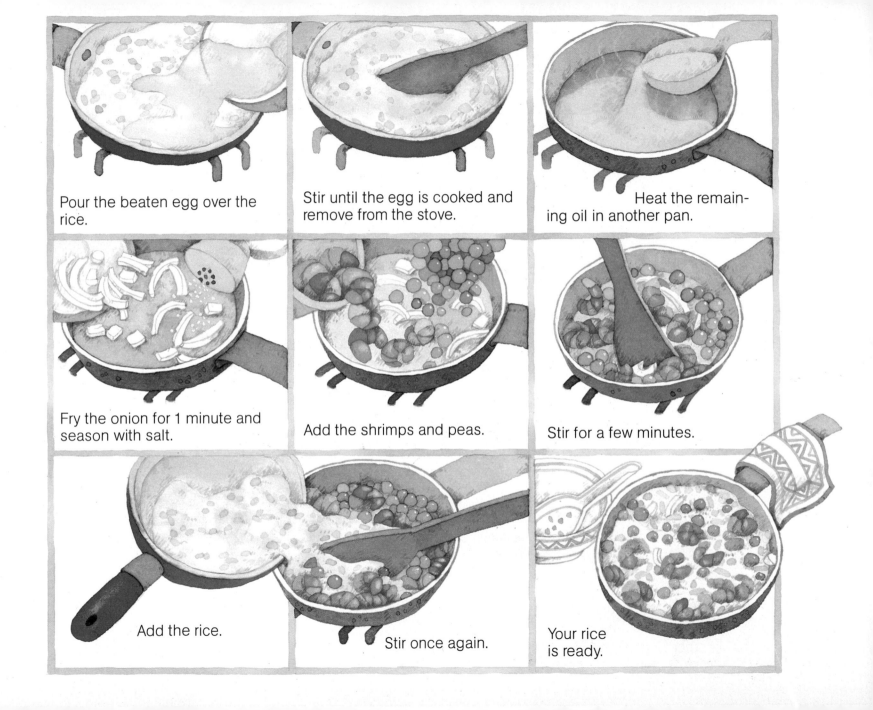

Pour the beaten egg over the rice.

Stir until the egg is cooked and remove from the stove.

Heat the remaining oil in another pan.

Fry the onion for 1 minute and season with salt.

Add the shrimps and peas.

Stir for a few minutes.

Add the rice.

Stir once again.

Your rice is ready.

Risotto Milanese Style

For 6 people:

500 g white rice

1 stock cube

salt and pepper

pinch of saffron

1 onion, chopped

80 g unsalted butter

2 tablespoons boiled beef
 marrow (optional)

50 g grated parmesan cheese

In a bowl, mix the saffron with
2 tablespoons of stock.

Heat the beef marrow and
some butter in a pan.

Add the onion and fry.

Add the rice and stir for a few seconds.

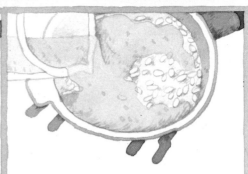

Pour the remaining stock into the pan.

Cover and cook for 10 minutes over a low heat.

Season with salt and pepper, add the saffron and mix well.

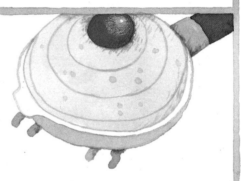

Cover for five minutes until the rice is cooked.

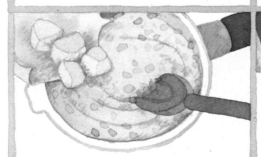

Add the remaining butter.

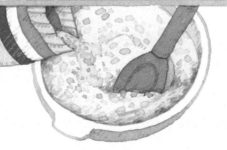

Sprinkle with parmesan cheese.

Serve your risotto piping hot.

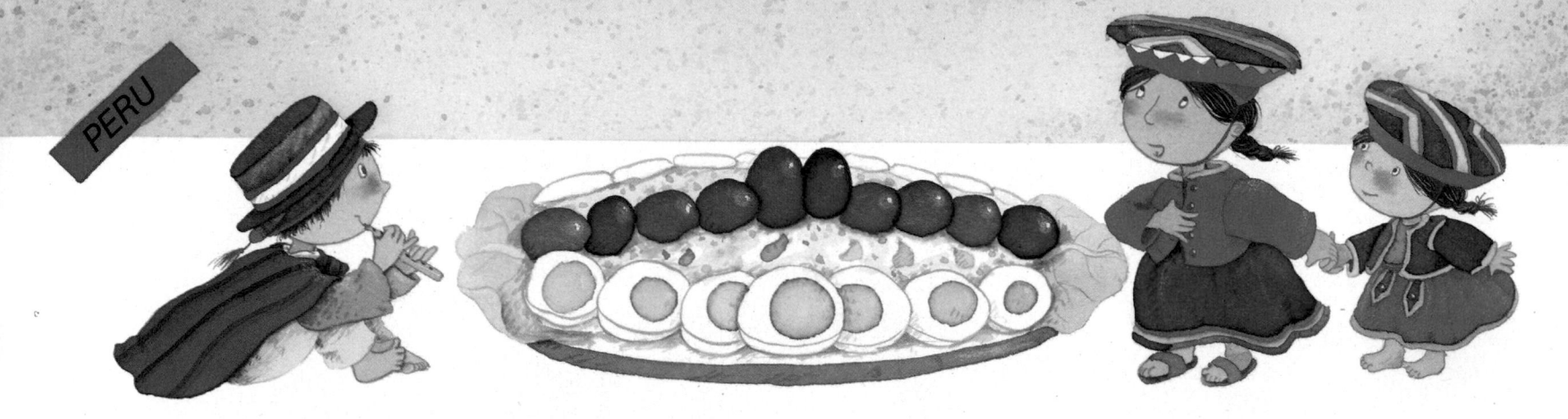

Potatoes a la Huancaina

For 5 people:

10 medium sized potatoes, peeled and boiled

100 g sieved cottage cheese

3 hard-boiled egg yolks

2 tablespoons chilli powder

salt and pepper

3 tablespoons sunflower oil

1 tablespoon unsweetened evaporated milk

5 hard-boiled eggs to be sliced

lemon juice

½ chopped onion

10 stoned black olives

a few washed lettuce leaves

Boil some water and cook the onion for a few minutes.

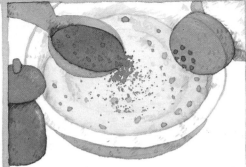

Mash the egg yolks with a fork, add them to the cottage cheese.

Add the chilli, salt and pepper...

...then the oil, evaporated milk and lemon juice.

Mix up well and add the drained onion.

Cut the potatoes into slices and arrange them on a dish.

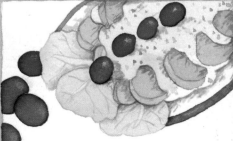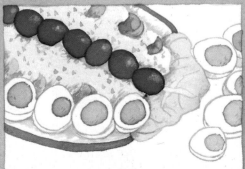

Cover with the sauce.

Garnish with the lettuce and olives...

...and slices of hard-boiled egg.

BURMA

Chutney Rice

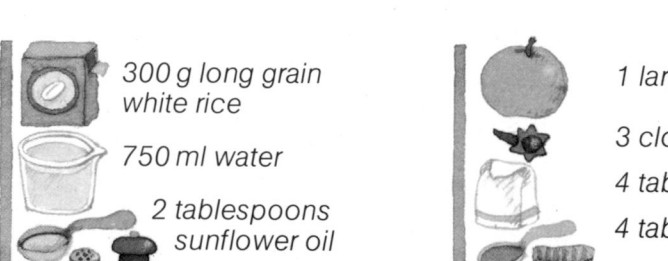

300 g long grain white rice

750 ml water

2 tablespoons sunflower oil

salt and pepper

1 large cooking apple

3 cloves

4 tablespoons sugar

4 tablespoons wine vinegar

4 tablespoons raisins

Heat the oil in a large pan.

Add the rice and stir for 1 minute, season with salt and pepper.

Add all the water and cover the pan.

Cook for 15 minutes over a low heat.

In the meantime, peel the apple…

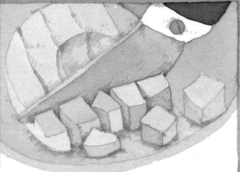

…and chop it into pieces.

Pour the sugar, vinegar and salt into another pan over a low heat, add the cloves, apple and raisins.

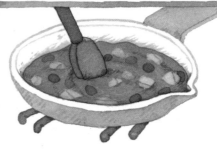

Cook your sauce slowly until it thickens.

Allow the chutney to cool.

When the rice is cooked, put it in a dish…

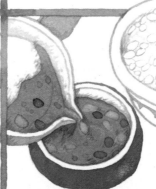

…and serve the chutney on the side.

Tomato Quiche

For 6 people:

250 g ready-made
short crust pastry

150 g double cream

150 g grated
gruyere or cheddar
cheese

4 big tomatoes

4 eggs

150 ml milk

parsley

salt and pepper

½ clove garlic, chopped

a buttered piece of greaseproof
paper

Roll out the
dough on a floured table

Grease a pie dish...

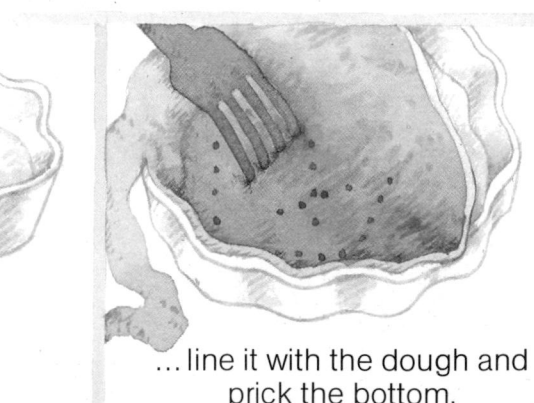

...line it with the dough and
prick the bottom.

Scald the tomatoes in water for 1 minute.

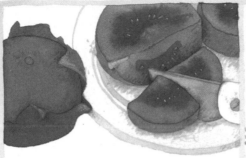

Drain them, peel and chop them into pieces.

Chop the parsley in a glass with scissors.

Mix the eggs, parsley, garlic and tomatoes in a big salad bowl.

Add the cheese, cream, milk, salt and pepper.

Beat with a fork until well blended.

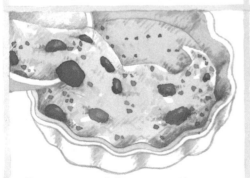

Pour your mixture over the dough.

Cook the quiche in the oven at 200°C for 60 minutes.

Serve immediately...

Hutspot or Boiled Beef

For 6 people:

500 g lean stewing beef

500 g carrots

250 g onions

1 kg potatoes

1 stock cube

salt and pepper

Heat 2 litres of water in a large pan.

Add the stock cube and the beef.

Simmer over a low heat for 2 hours.

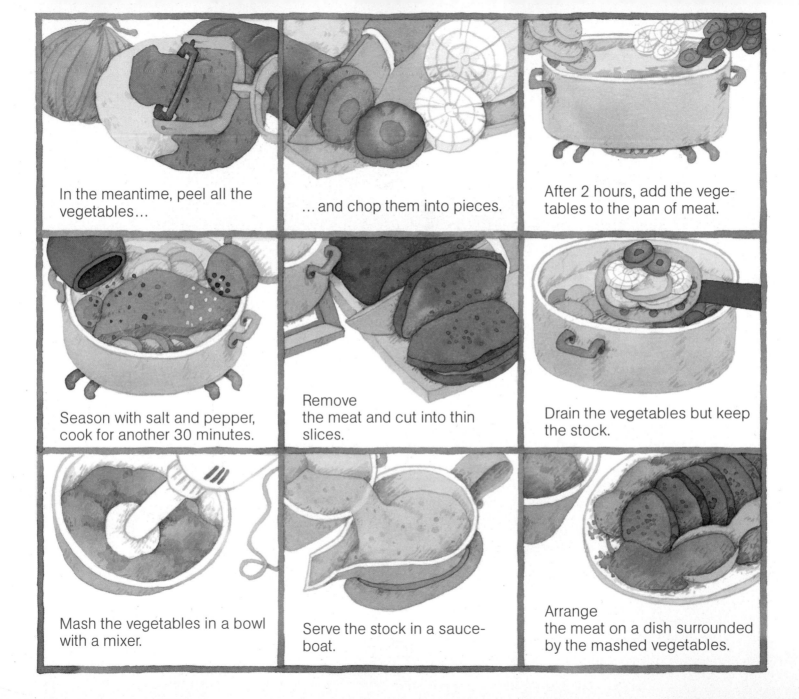

In the meantime, peel all the vegetables...

... and chop them into pieces.

After 2 hours, add the vegetables to the pan of meat.

Season with salt and pepper, cook for another 30 minutes.

Remove the meat and cut into thin slices.

Drain the vegetables but keep the stock.

Mash the vegetables in a bowl with a mixer.

Serve the stock in a sauceboat.

Arrange the meat on a dish surrounded by the mashed vegetables.

Spinach a la Manchega

 500 g washed spinach

1 l water

1 medium onion, chopped

100 g tomatoes

2 tablespoons wine vinegar

1 clove garlic

salt and cumin powder

olive oil

Boil the water in a saucepan.

Add a pinch of salt and cook the spinach for a few minutes.

Scald the tomatoes for 1 minute to peel them.

Cut them into slices.

Heat the oil in a big pan…

…and fry the onion and tomato slices.

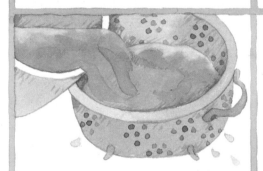

Drain the cooked spinach in a colander…

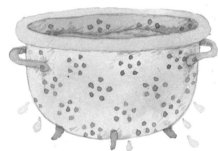

…thoroughly.

Add to the pan.

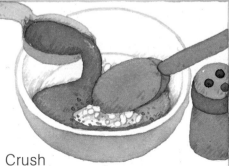

Crush the garlic in a bowl, add the cumin and vinegar.

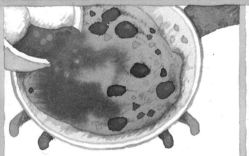

Add the sauce to the spinach and simmer over a low heat for 5 minutes.

Serve your spinach piping hot…

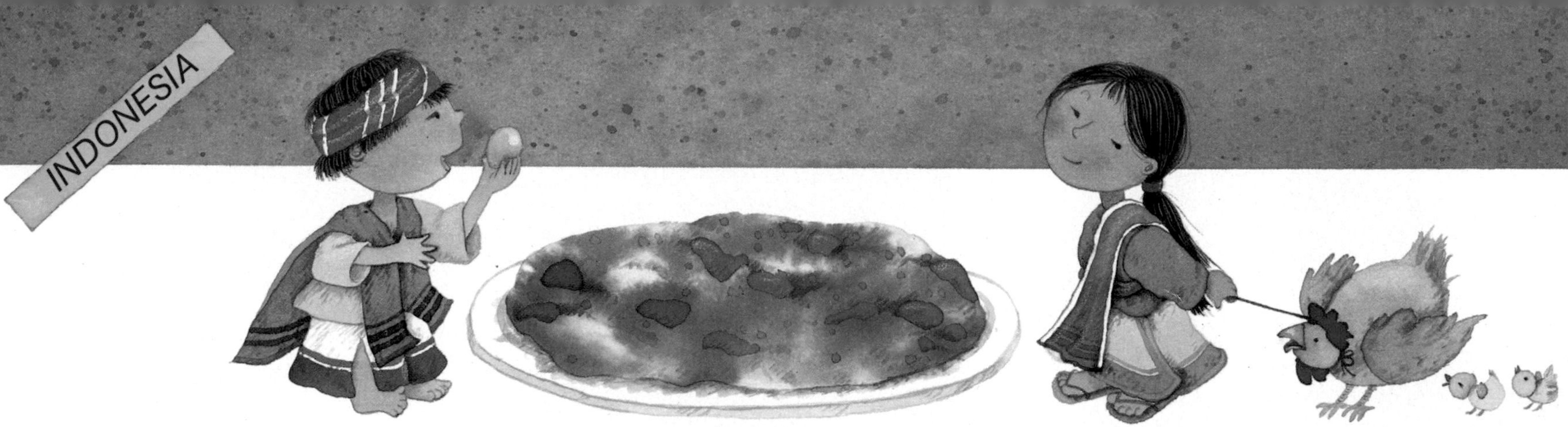

Scrambled Eggs with Tomato

6 medium tomatoes

4 eggs

2 small onions, diced

1 chilli, chopped

salt and pepper

oil

Wash the tomatoes

Chop them into slices.

Heat the oil in a pan.

Cook the onions for a few minutes.

Add the tomatoes and the chilli.

Simmer for 3 minutes.

Break the eggs into the pan

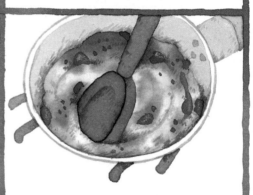
Stir well.

Season with salt and pepper.

Cook for another 3 minutes.

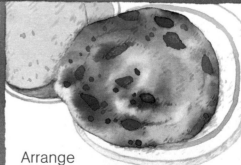
Arrange your scrambled eggs on an attractive dish.

Enchiladas

For 6 people :

- 250 g plain flour
- 4 eggs
- 500 ml milk
- salt, pepper

- paprika, chilli powder
- sunflower oil
- 250 g cooked ham
- 1 medium onion
- 1 clove garlic, chopped

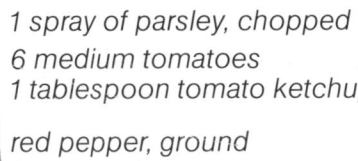

- 1 spray of parsley, chopped
- 6 medium tomatoes
- 1 tablespoon tomato ketchup
- red pepper, ground
- marjoram
- 100 g cooking cheese cut into strips

Prepare a pancake batter with flour, 3 eggs, salt and ⅔ of milk.

In an oiled frying pan, pour a ladleful of batter and cook your pancake.

Once cooked, flip it over and cook the other side, then take it out of the pan. Proceed the same way for the other pancakes.

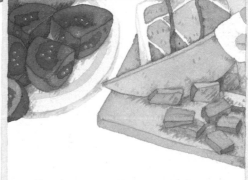

Blend the remaining milk, egg, chilli, paprika, salt and pepper. Dip your pancakes in the mixture. Brown them on both sides in the pan.

Dice the tomatoes and ham.

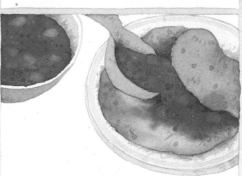

In another pan, brown the onion, garlic, ham, tomatoes and parsley. Add ketchup and season with salt, pepper, red pepper and marjoram.

Fill each pancake with the stuffing and fold it.

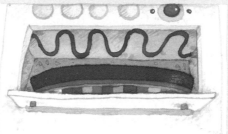

Arrange them in a baking dish. Sprinkle with cheese.

Cook under the grill

until the cheese melts.

Hints for Healthy Eating

Did you know that all the foods we eat contain everything we need to make the cells from which our bodies are built?

There are millions of cells, all of which are mostly water, but which also contain a mixture of proteins, fats and carbohydrates, as well as vitamins and mineral salts.

The different contents of the cells need to be provided from the food we eat, and we can divide this food into the same three main categories: proteins, fats, and carbohydrates.

Body building foods:

Provide *protein* that keeps your body going, and helps it grow big and strong:
milk · cheese · eggs · meat · fish · cereals · vegetables...

Energy-giving foods:

Provide the energy needed for all physical activity.

Fats:
butter · oil · margarine · cream · cheese · walnuts · chocolate · sausages...

Glucides:
sugar · honey · jam · fruit · sweet vegetables · flour · bread · rice...

Substances that help promote the good use of other foods:

They are indispensable to your body as they provide *vitamins:*
fruit · vegetables · dairy products...

and *mineral salts,* the most important being calcium (for your bones and teeth):
dairy products (especially cheese) · lentils · certain fruit

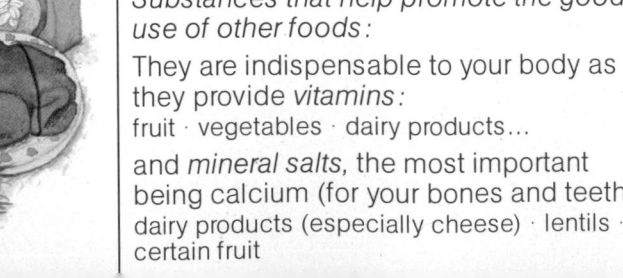

and *iron* (for your blood):
liver · egg yolks · green vegetables · walnuts · hazelnuts · wholemeal bread...

Water is indispensable, so do not forget to drink some between meals...

Now, all you have to learn is how to balance your food intake by eating food from each category every day. Try to vary your meals, even if some dishes are not as appealing as others. Another piece of advice... take your time, and slowly chew each mouthful of food. This will help your digestion...

Bear in mind that sugar is not good for your teeth. Try to avoid too many sweets and fizzy drinks.

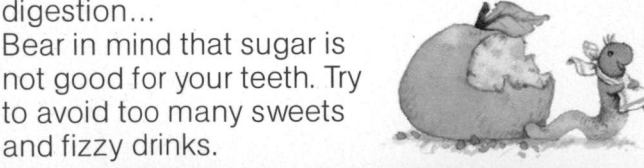

Food for All Children

In this book you will find recipes that children love from countries all over the world.

But many children in the world spend a lot of time thinking about food because they do not have enough to eat. They often have few of the other things we all need to live as well.

Have you thought what these are? Just like you, children all over the world need a roof to provide shelter from the weather, a family to love and who loves them. Children need a school where they can learn to read and write, a doctor or nurse in their town or village in case they are ill. These are called basic needs. Can you imagine living without them?

Many children in the world do. The United Nations Children's Fund (known as UNICEF) is here to help. UNICEF works to make sure that all children, wherever they are, have their basic needs met.

Today it is in Africa, Asia and Latin America that children need the most help. UNICEF helps families to grow more food. It helps villages to dig wells so that everyone – grannies, grandpas, mothers, fathers and children – have clean water to drink, wash and cook with.

UNICEF helps to make sure that there are enough doctors and nurses trained so that children can be cared for when they are ill.

When a family does not have all its basic needs, life can be very difficult. But if there is a war, or a drought or a very bad storm which causes floods, the poorest families can lose everything they have. This is another time when UNICEF is ready to help. It can rush in emergency food, medical supplies and other things to help children and their families.

Did you know that UNICEF has earned money from selling this book? This money is now helping children in need all over the world.

This cookery book also offers you a chance to try making and eating the favourite meals of children all over the world. When you are looking at each recipe, think of the children who live in that country. You will then be sharing a moment with children from all over the world.

Go on – try chakchoukas from Tunisia, or empanadas from Chile – try a recipe that you have never tasted before!

Chakchouka

3 large green peppers

2 onions

8 small washed tomatoes

olive oil

salt and pepper

cayenne pepper

6 eggs

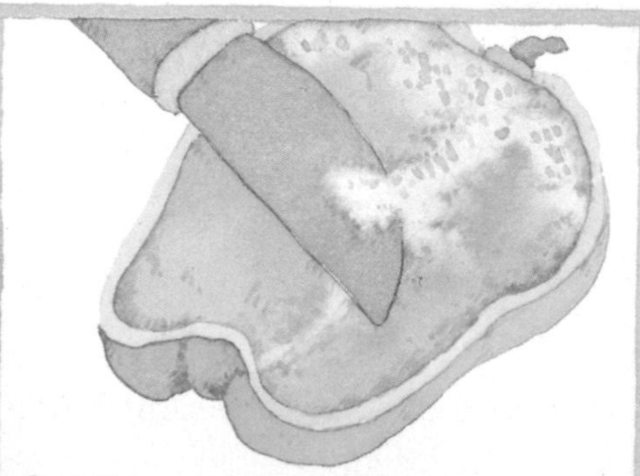

Cut the green peppers in half and remove the seeds.

Chop into thin strips.

Peel the onions under running water...

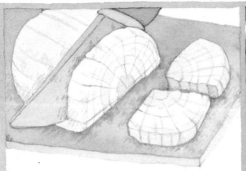

... slice them.

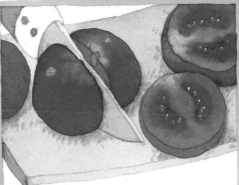

Cut the tomatoes in half.

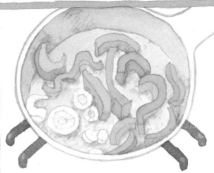

Heat the oil in a pan and add the onions and green peppers.

Season with salt, pepper and cayenne pepper and cook over a low heat.

Add the tomatoes and cook until the green peppers are tender.

Break the eggs in a bowl and beat (like an omelette).

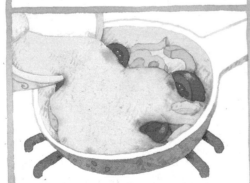

Pour the eggs into the pan...

... as soon as they are scrambled, your dish is ready.

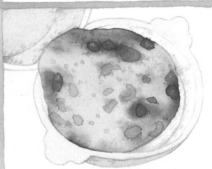

Serve it piping hot.

Empanadas – Meat Turnovers

For 6 people:

500 g plain flour

½ teaspoon baking powder,   2 eggs

1 tablespoon luke-warm milk
a pinch of salt

200 g softened butter

250 g minced meat

2 onions, chopped
1 clove garlic, chopped
1 dried red pepper, crushed

2 hard-boiled eggs, chopped

8 stoned green olives

50 g raisins

paprika, marjoram

sunflower oil

a 10 cm bowl

1 beaten egg

Stir the flour and the baking powder in a bowl and make a well in the centre.

Pour in the milk, eggs and salt, mix well.

Add the butter to obtain a smooth dough.

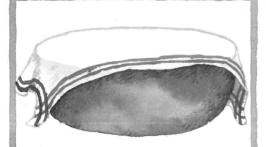

Let the dough stand for 2 hours.

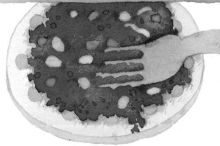

To prepare the stuffing, mix the meat, onions, garlic and red pepper.

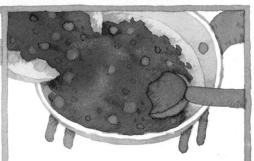

Heat the oil in a pan and cook the stuffing in it.

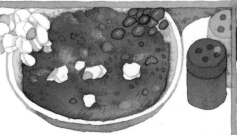

Let it cool and add the chopped eggs, olives, raisins, paprika and marjoram.

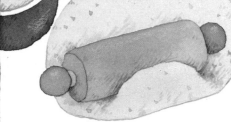

Roll out the dough as if you were making a pie.

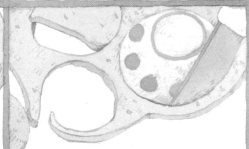

Use a 10 cm bowl and cut out circles.

Cover each half-circle with the stuffing. Brush the edges with the beaten egg.

Fold each circle in two and press on the sides.

Brown your turnovers on both sides in the oil and serve them.

Salzburg Soufflé

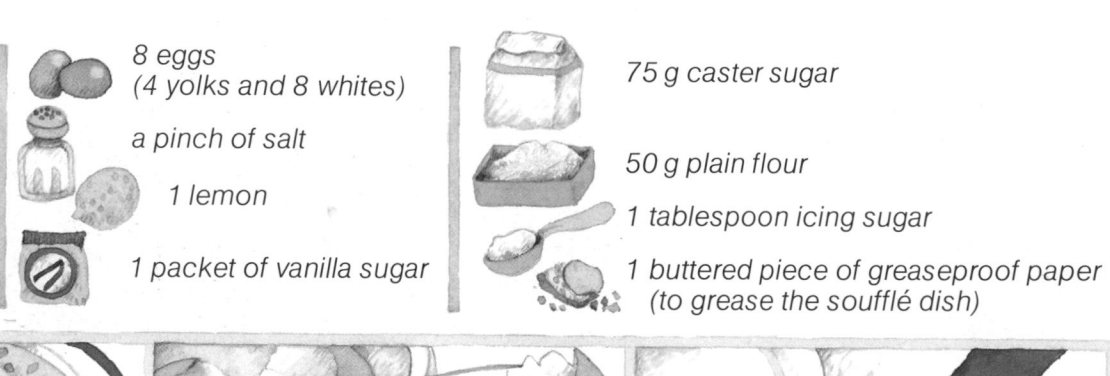

8 eggs
(4 yolks and 8 whites)

a pinch of salt

1 lemon

1 packet of vanilla sugar

75 g caster sugar

50 g plain flour

1 tablespoon icing sugar

1 buttered piece of greaseproof paper
(to grease the soufflé dish)

Grate the lemon rind.

Separate the
egg whites from the yolks, place
4 yolks in a bowl.

Whisk the yolks with the
lemon rind.

Add a pinch of salt to the egg whites and whisk until stiff.

Blend in the sugar and vanilla sugar and continue to whisk.

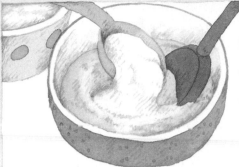

Mix a spoonful of egg whites in with the yolks…

…and then gently fold in the remaining whites.

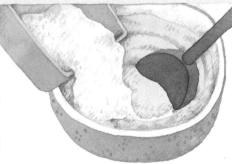

Sieve the flour and add to the mixture.

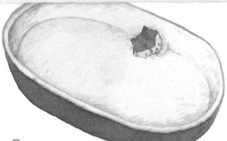

Grease a soufflé dish and turn the oven on to 250°C.

Pour in your mixture in three separate heaps…

…and place in the oven for 15 minutes.

Remove the soufflé when golden and sprinkle with icing sugar.

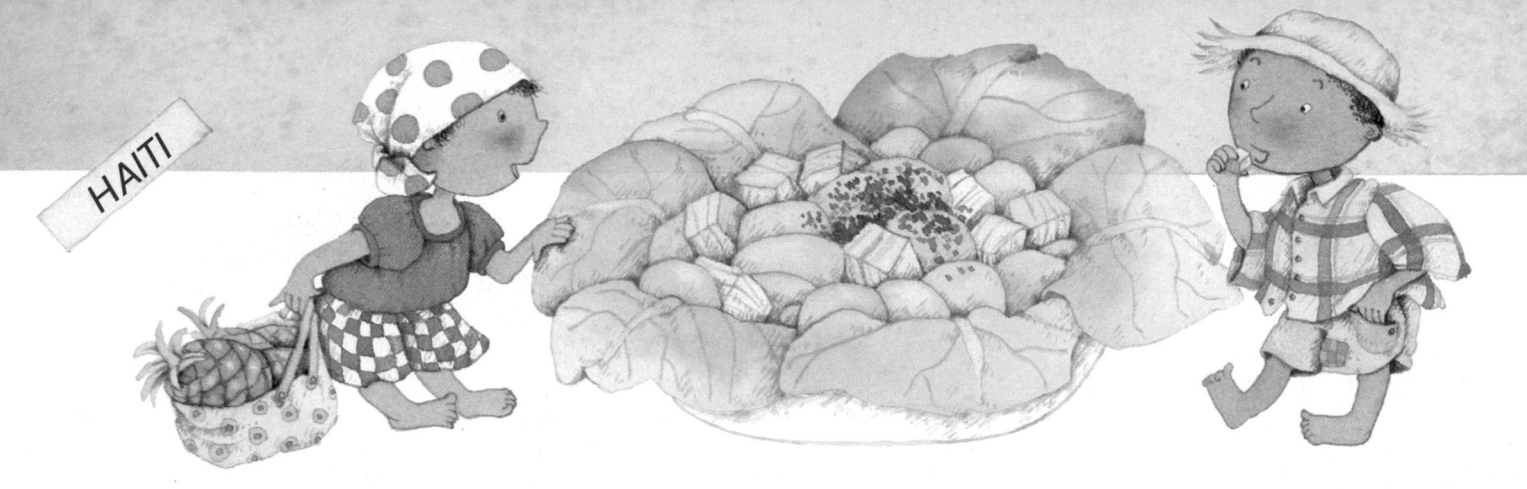

Avocado Salad with Pineapple

1 large ripe avocado

4 slices pineapple, fresh or tinned

washed lettuce leaves

6 teaspoons olive oil

2 teaspoons lemon juice

salt, parsley

Cut the avocado in half and remove the stone.

Scoop out the flesh with a teaspoon.

Cut the flesh into small pieces.

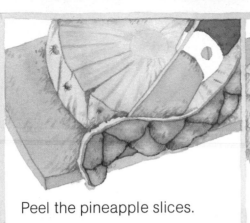

Peel the pineapple slices.

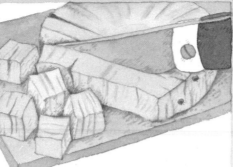

Cut each slice of pineapple into cubes.

Put the avocado and pineapple in a salad bowl.

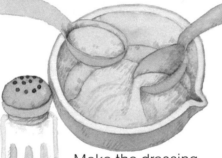

Make the dressing with the olive oil, lemon juice and a pinch of salt.

Mix up with a fork…

…and pour over the fruit.

Line a dish with the lettuce leaves…

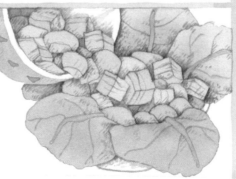

…and cover them with the contents of the bowl.

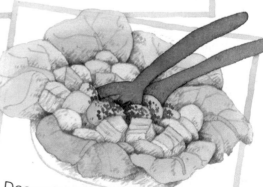

Decorate with parsley. Your salad is ready…

Bircher Müesli

2 small cartons of natural yoghurt.

100 ml single cream

50 g porridge oats

seedless raisins

juice of 1 lemon

4 teaspoons caster sugar

1 large apple

1 banana

hazelnuts

Mix the porridge oats with the raisins.

Add a little water…

let it swell for an hour.

Add the lemon juice and sugar.

Pour in the cream and yoghurt, stir well.

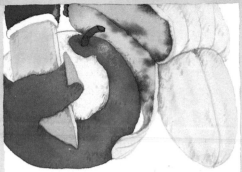

Peel the apple and the banana.

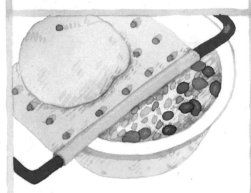

Grate the apple.

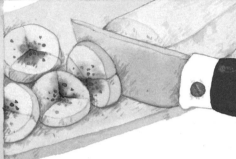

Slice the banana.

Grind the hazelnuts.

Add the fruit to the müesli and mix once again.

Chill the mixture overnight if possible

...bircher müesli is delicious for breakfast.

Mango Clown

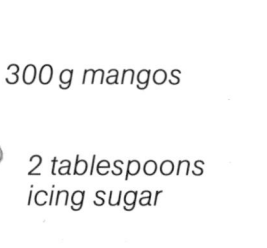
300 g mangos

2 tablespoons
icing sugar

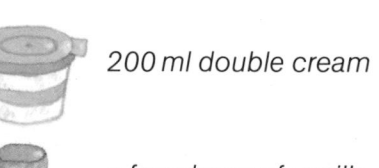
200 ml double cream

a few drops of vanilla
essence

Peel the mangos.

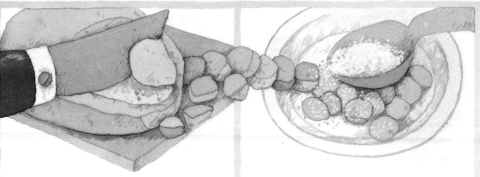

Cut them into small pieces.

Sprinkle with icing-sugar.

Whip the cream until stiff.

Flavour with the vanilla essence.

Mix carefully.

Place the dishes of cream and mango in the refrigerator.

Remove from refrigerator shortly before serving.

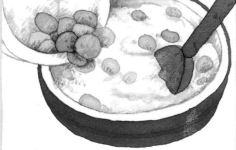

Carefully blend together mangos and cream.

The clown is ready!

Frozen Lemon Mousse

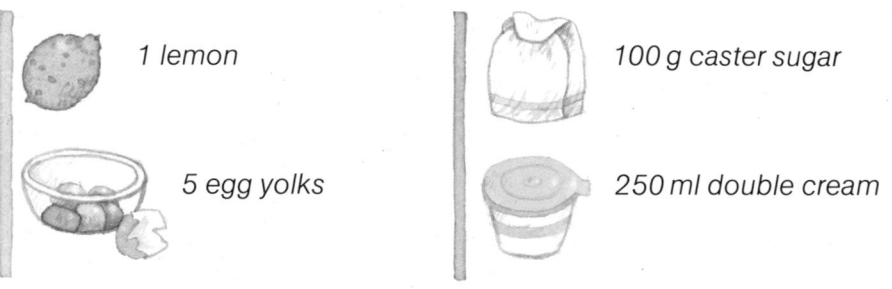

1 lemon

100 g caster sugar

5 egg yolks

250 ml double cream

Wash the lemon thoroughly and dry it.

Put the egg yolks and sugar into a freezer-proof bowl.

Whisk the mixture until it is fluffy.

Whip the cream in a separate bowl until stiff.

Carefully fold the cream into the egg yolks.

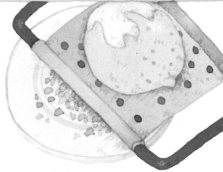

Grate the lemon rind finely.

Cut the lemon in half and squeeze out the juice.

Add the lemon rind and juice to the mixture, mix together gently.

Place the mousse in the freezer for 3 or 4 hours.

Remove it shortly before dessert time.

Baked Bananas

4 big bananas

40 g butter

2 tablespoons honey

lemon juice

200 ml soured cream

Peel the bananas.

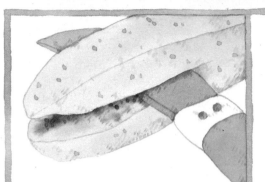
Cut them in half, lengthways.

Turn the oven on to 250°C.

Grease a baking dish.

Arrange your banana halves in a dish.

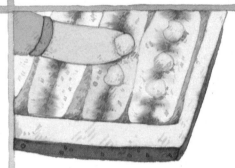
Dot with knobs of butter.

Spread the honey and lemon juice over the bananas.

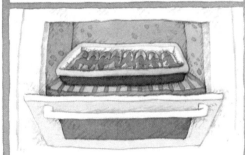
Bake for 40 minutes.

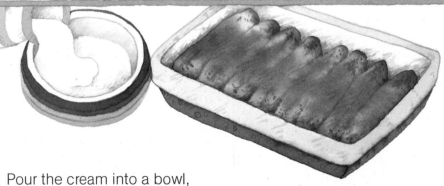
Pour the cream into a bowl, and serve it with your baked bananas.

Queen of Puddings

400 ml milk

25 g unsalted butter
grated rind of ½ lemon

2 eggs

50 g caster sugar

75 g fresh breadcrumbs

½ jar of raspberry or strawberry jam

Gently heat the milk, butter and lemon rind.

Separate the egg yolks from the egg whites.

Whisk the yolks and half the sugar and pour in the milk.

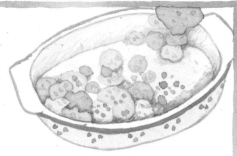

Grease a baking dish and sprinkle it with the breadcrumbs.

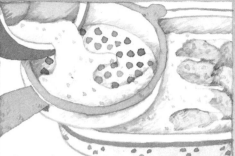

Pour the milk mixture over it through a large holed colander.

Leave it to stand for 15 minutes and turn the oven on to 180° C.

Bake for 30 minutes.

Warm the jam in a small saucepan.

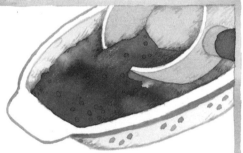

Take the pudding out of the oven and spread the jam over the top.

Whisk the egg whites and remaining sugar until stiff. This is called meringue.

Pile the meringue over the pudding and bake for 15 minutes …

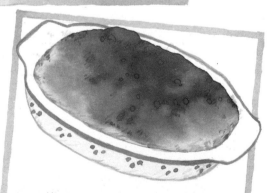

… until the meringue is lightly brown.

Mango and Banana Sundae

1 fresh or tinned mango

2 bananas

2 tablespoons lemon juice

4 tablespoons orange juice

500 ml vanilla ice-cream

Peel the mango.

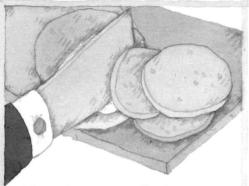

Chop the mango finely.

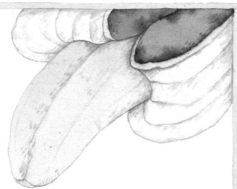

Peel the bananas.

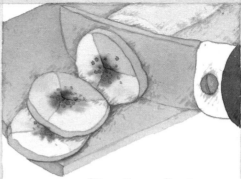

Slice them finely.

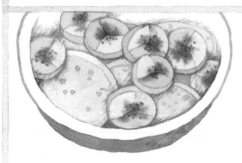

Put the fruit into a large bowl.

Add the lemon and orange juice…

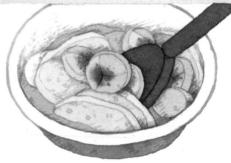

… mix carefully.

Serve the ice-cream in sundae dishes.

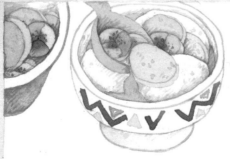

Cover with the mixed fruit.

It's very good, you'll see…

CANADA

Scones

125 g plain flour

½ teaspoon baking powder

30 g caster sugar

30 g unsalted, softened butter

30 g seedless raisins

4 tablespoons milk

unsalted butter

your favourite jam

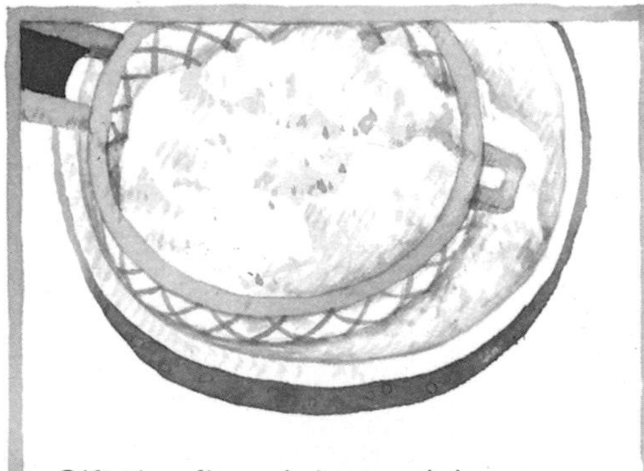

Sift the flour into a mixing bowl.

Pour in the sugar.

Add the butter in pieces. Rub it into the flour.

Flour the raisins by adding them to a little flour in a sieve and shaking them over the sink.

Add them to the flour and butter mixture.

Mix with your fingers while gradually adding the milk.

Turn the oven on to 250°C (hot oven).

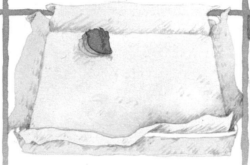

Line a baking tray with aluminium foil and grease it slightly.

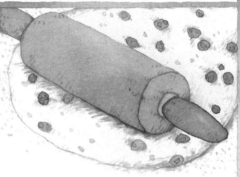

On a floured table, roll out your dough to 1 cm thick.

Cut out triangles with a knife.

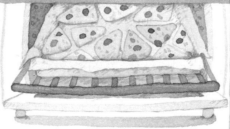

Arrange them on the baking tray and cook for 5 to 7 minutes.

Serve your scones lukewarm with butter and jam.

Pancakes

For 20 pancakes:

250 g plain flour

60 g caster sugar

½ teaspoon cinnamon

1 pinch salt

5 eggs

2 tablespoons oil

750 ml milk

100 g unsalted butter

juice of 5 oranges

3 tablespoons cocoa powder

5 tablespoons icing sugar

Mix the flour, sugar, salt and cinnamon in a bowl.	Make a well in the centre and break the eggs into it.	Beat the mixture.

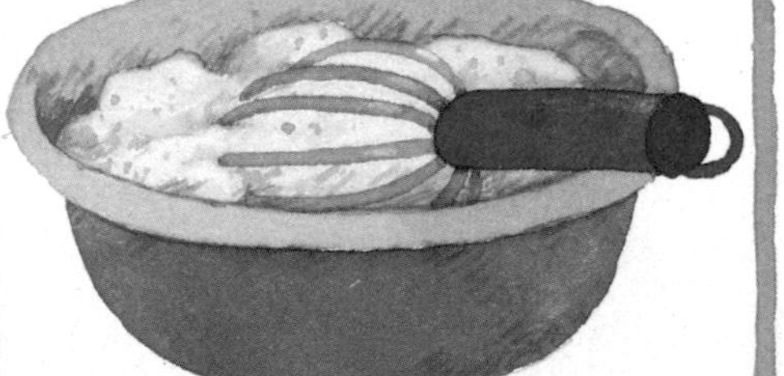

Add the oil and stir well.

Gradually blend in the milk, beat well or use electric mixer.

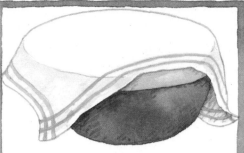

Cover the bowl with a clean tea towel and leave to stand for 2 hours.

Heat some butter in a frying pan over a medium heat.

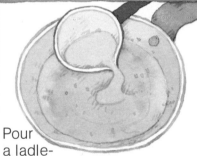

Pour a ladleful of batter into the middle of the pan, grasp the pan in both hands to spread the batter evenly.

Once the pancake is cooked on one side flip it over with a flat wooden spatula.

Let it cook and sprinkle with some orange juice…

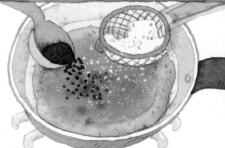

… add ½ teaspoon of cocoa and 1 teaspoon of icing sugar using a fine sieve.

Put the pancake on a warm plate and prepare the others the same way.

Home-Made Bread

250 g plain flour

½ teaspoon salt

1 level teaspoon dried yeast

150 ml tepid water

Mix the yeast in the tepid water.

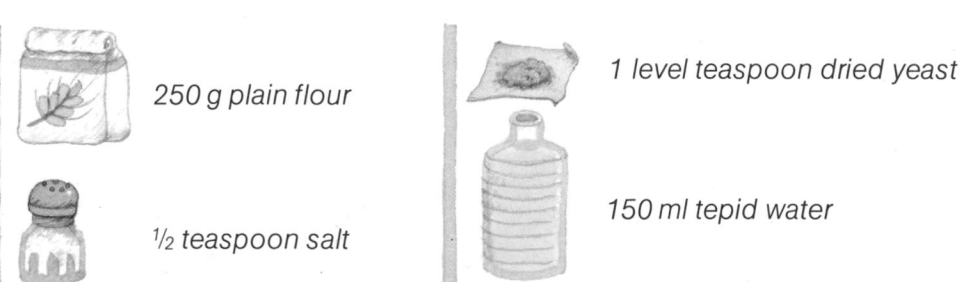

Mix the flour and salt in a bowl and make a well in the centre.

Pour the yeast in the centre and rub until it forms a ball.

Knead well. The dough should not stick to your fingers.

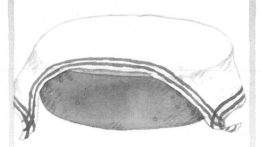

Cover the bowl with a damp tea towel and allow to rise in a warm place (20° C).

After an hour, the dough should have doubled in size.

Knead the dough again and press it into a long shape.

Grease a baking tray and turn the oven on to 250° C.

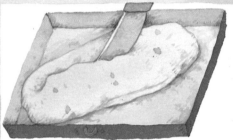

Put the dough on the tray and score with a knife.

Leave to stand for 30 minutes…

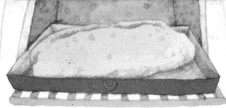

… bake for 30 minutes.

You are a baker!

Orange Cake

For 6 people:

4 eggs

125 g softened unsalted butter

200 g caster sugar

125 g sieved plain flour

1 teaspoon baking powder

2 medium oranges

For the sauce:

150 g sugar

250 ml water

Separate the egg whites from the yolks. Whisk the yolks with the butter.

Add the sugar and whisk again.

Pour in the flour and stir.

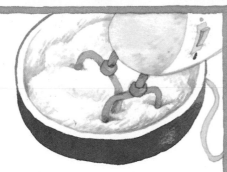

Whisk the egg whites until they are stiff.

Fold them carefully into the cake mixture.

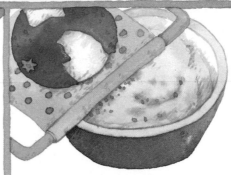

Add the finely grated rind of 2 oranges.

Pour the mixture into a greased tin – we suggest a 20 cm tin or use one with a fun shape.

Cook the cake in a medium oven (200° C) for 45 minutes.

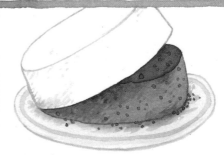

As soon as it is cooked, remove the tin and cool on a cake rack.

Boil the water and sugar for 5 minutes.

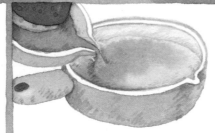

Take the pan off the heat and add the juice of 2 oranges.

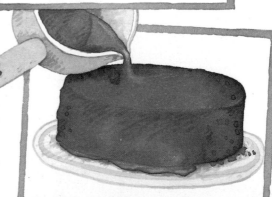

Pour the sauce over the lukewarm cake.

Mantecados – Cinnamon Biscuits

250 g sieved plain flour

125 g caster sugar

rind of ½ lemon

100 ml sunflower oil

ground cinnamon

Put the flour into a large bowl.

Make a well in the centre.

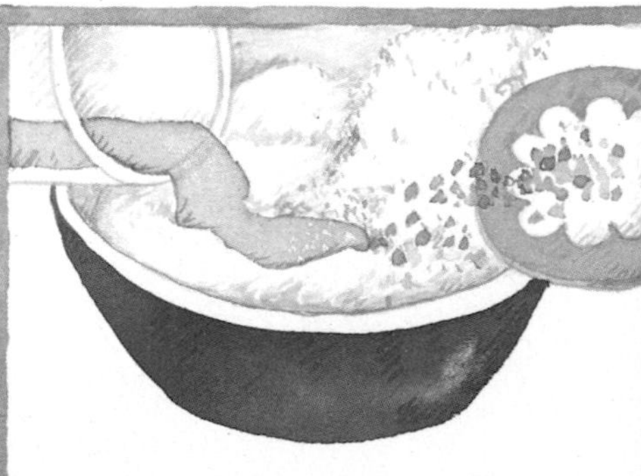

Add the oil, sugar and finely grated lemon rind.

Mix the dough together.

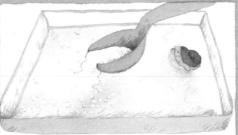
Grease a baking tray, sprinkle with some flour.

Make into small balls and flatten a little.

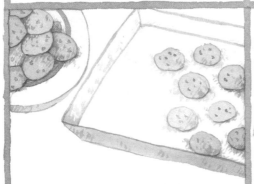
Arrange them on the tray.

Leave to stand for 20 minutes.

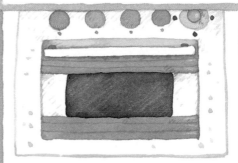
Turn the oven on to 200° C.

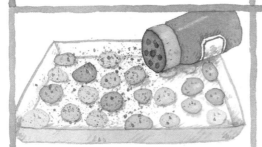
Then sprinkle the biscuits with cinnamon.

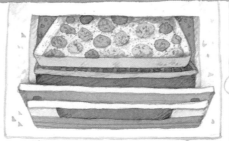
Bake for 20 minutes…

…and the mantecados are ready…

Hazelnut Cake

For 6 people:

6 eggs

250 g brown sugar

10 tablespoons milk

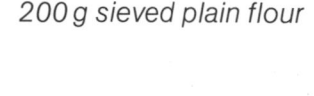 200 g sieved plain flour

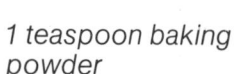 1 teaspoon baking powder

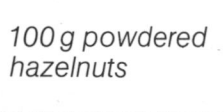 100 g powdered hazelnuts

Separate the egg whites from the yolks.

Put the yolks, sugar and milk into a bowl.

Mix well.

Continue to whisk and add the flour and hazelnuts.

Turn the oven on to 200° C.

Whisk the egg whites until stiff.

Fold them gently into the cake mixture.

Grease a round cake tin – we suggest a 20 cm tin or use one with a fun shape.

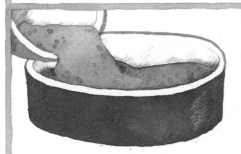

Pour in the cake mixture.

Bake the cake for 45 minutes.

Remove the cake from the tin when it is cool.

Ful-Sudani – Peanut Macaroons

110 g peanuts, unsalted

1 egg white

1 pinch of salt

160 g caster sugar

1/2 teaspoon vanilla essence

greaseproof paper

Brown the peanuts under the grill.

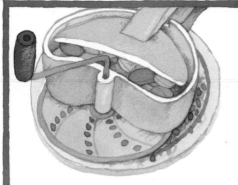

Grind them.

Whisk the egg white with a pinch of salt until stiff.

Add the sugar and whisk again...

...then add the peanuts.

Put the greaseproof paper on a baking tray.

Grease it a little.

Put small heaps of the mixture on the paper.

Cook at a low heat (180° C) until...

...macaroons are golden.

Jam Biscuits

200 g softened unsalted butter

1 egg white

125 g caster sugar

1 teaspoon lemon juice

1 pinch of salt

350 g sieved plain flour

raspberry jam or redcurrant jelly

icing sugar

a 7 cm diameter pot
greaseproof paper

Mix the butter and sugar.

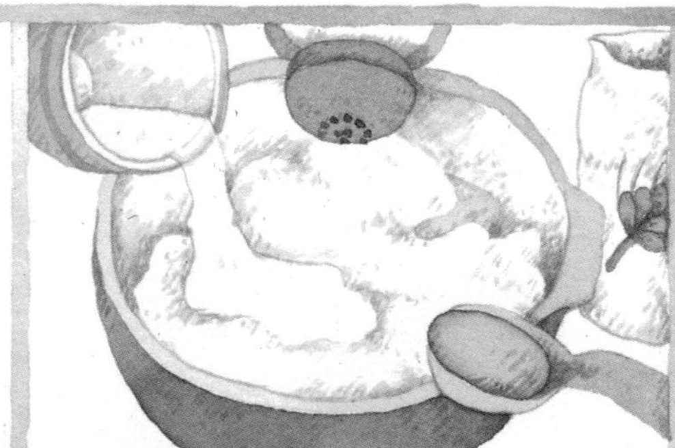

Add the egg white, lemon juice, salt and flour.

Mix well and leave to stand for one hour.

Roll out the dough (3 mm thick) on a floured table.

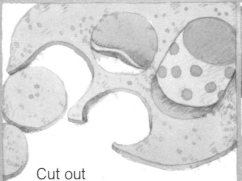

Cut out circles using the pot…

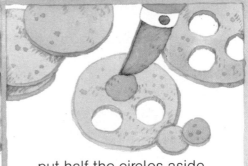

…put half the circles aside and cut 3 small holes in each remaining circle.

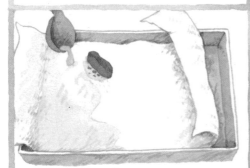

Line a baking tray with greaseproof paper.

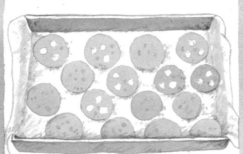

Arrange all the circles on it.

Bake them in a medium oven (230° C).

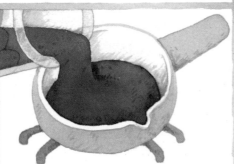

Warm the jam or jelly in a pan.

Spread it over the circles without holes and sandwich with the other circles pressing gently.

Sprinkle your biscuits with icing sugar.

Betűsütemény – Letter Biscuits

180 g sieved plain flour

90 g caster sugar

60 g softened unsalted butter

1 egg

vanilla essence

For the icing:

200 g icing sugar

2 tablespoons lemon juice

1 packet of small chocolate sweets

Mix the flour, sugar and butter in a bowl.

Add the egg and a few drops of vanilla essence.

Turn the oven on to 200°C.

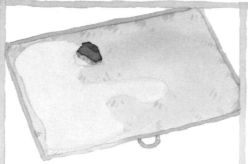

Grease a baking tray.

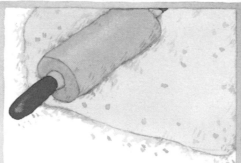

Roll out the dough (1 cm thick) on a floured table.

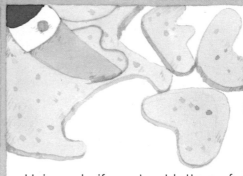

Using a knife, cut out letters of your choice.

Arrange the letters on the tray.

Put the tray in the oven for 10-15 minutes then take it out.

Pour the lemon juice in a bowl and add the icing sugar gradually.

Using a brush, cover the letters with the icing…

…decorate with the sweets.

Now write anything you want!

Österreichisches Komitee für UNICEF
Vienna International Centre — U.N.O. — Wagramer Strasse 22
A–1400 Wien — Tel.: 2360 Ext. 1557-59

Comité belge pour l'UNICEF
1, rue Joseph II — Boîte 9
B–1040 Bruxelles — Tel.: 230 5970

Belgisch Comite voor UNICEF
Josef II-Straat 1 – Bus 9
B–1040 Brussel — Tel.: 230 5970

Escritorio da UNICEF para cartões de saudações
Rua México 21, Grupo 902
20031 Rio de Janeiro, RJ, Brazil
Tel.: 240-5176

Canadian UNICEF Committee / Comité UNICEF Canada
443, Mount Pleasant Road
CND–Toronto, Ontario M4S 2L8 — Tel.: 482-4444

Jugoslovenski Nacionali Komitet za UNICEF
Lenjinov Bulevar 2, SIV 1
YU–11070 Novi Beograd — Tel.: 33 42 81

Dansk UNICEF Komite
Billedvej 8 — Frihavnen
DK–2100 København Ø — Tel.: 01/29 51 11

Suomen UNICEF-Yhdistys r.y.
Perttulantie 6
SF–00210 Helsinki — Tel.: 6927500

Finlands UNICEF-förening r.f.
Bertasvägen 6
SF–00210 Helsingfors — Tel.: 6927500

Comité français pour le FISE / UNICEF
35, rue Félicien-David
F–75781 Paris Cedex 16 — Tel.: 45 24 60 00 / 45 24 47 79

Deutsches Komitee für UNICEF
Steinfelder Gasse 9
D–5000 Köln 1 — Tel.: 16 00 80

Hellenic National Committee for UNICEF
Xenias St. 1
GR–11527 Athens — Tel.: 778 4223 / 778 32 08

Az Ensz Gyermekalap Magyar Nemzetti Bizottsága
Széchenyi Rakpart, 6
H–1054 Budapest 5 — Tel. 31 21 24 / 12 94 82

Irish National Committee for UNICEF
4, St. Andrew Street
IRL–Dublin 2 — Tel.: 77 08 43

Comitato Italiano per l'UNICEF
Piazza Marconi 25
I–00144 Roma EUR — Tel.: 59 17 975 / 59 17 976

Comité luxembourgeois pour l'UNICEF, a.s.b.l.
99, route d'Arlon
L–1140 Luxembourg — Tel.: 44 87 15 / 44 96 74

Stichting Nederlands Comité UNICEF
Bankastraat 128 — Postbus 85857
NL–2508 CN 's Gravenhage — Tel.: 50 16 00

FN-Sambandet I Norge (UN Association of Norway)
Langesgt 4
N–Oslo 1 — Tel.: 02/20 91 70

Polski Komitet Wspólpracy z UNICEF
Ul. Mokotowska, 39
PL–00551 Warszawa — Tel.: 29 06 76, Ext. 47 or 28 03 01

Comité português para a UNICEF
Pr. Dr. Fernando Amado, lote 568-1 (Zona j de Chelas)
P–1900 Lisboa — Tel.: 85 24 78 / 85 23 54

Asociación UNICEF — España
Mauricio Legendre, 36
E–28046 Madrid — Tel.: 733 24 15 / 733 40 00

Svenska UNICEF-Komitten
Asögatan 149 — Box 111 14
S–100 61 Stockholm — Tel.: 714 54 60

Schweizerisches Komitee für UNICEF
Comité suisse pour l'UNICEF
Comitato svizzero per l'UNICEF
Werdstrasse 36
CH–8021 Zürich 1 — Tel.: 242 70 80 / 241 18 06 / 241 40 30

UNICEF Türkiye Milli Komitesi
Abdullah Cevdet Sok. 22/10 — Cankaya
TR–Ankara — Tel.: 38 17 45

United Kingdom Committee for UNICEF
55, Lincoln's Inn Fields
GB–London WC2A 3NB

United States Committee for UNICEF
331 East 38th Street
USA–New York, N.Y. 10016 — Tel.: 686 55 22